I0712132

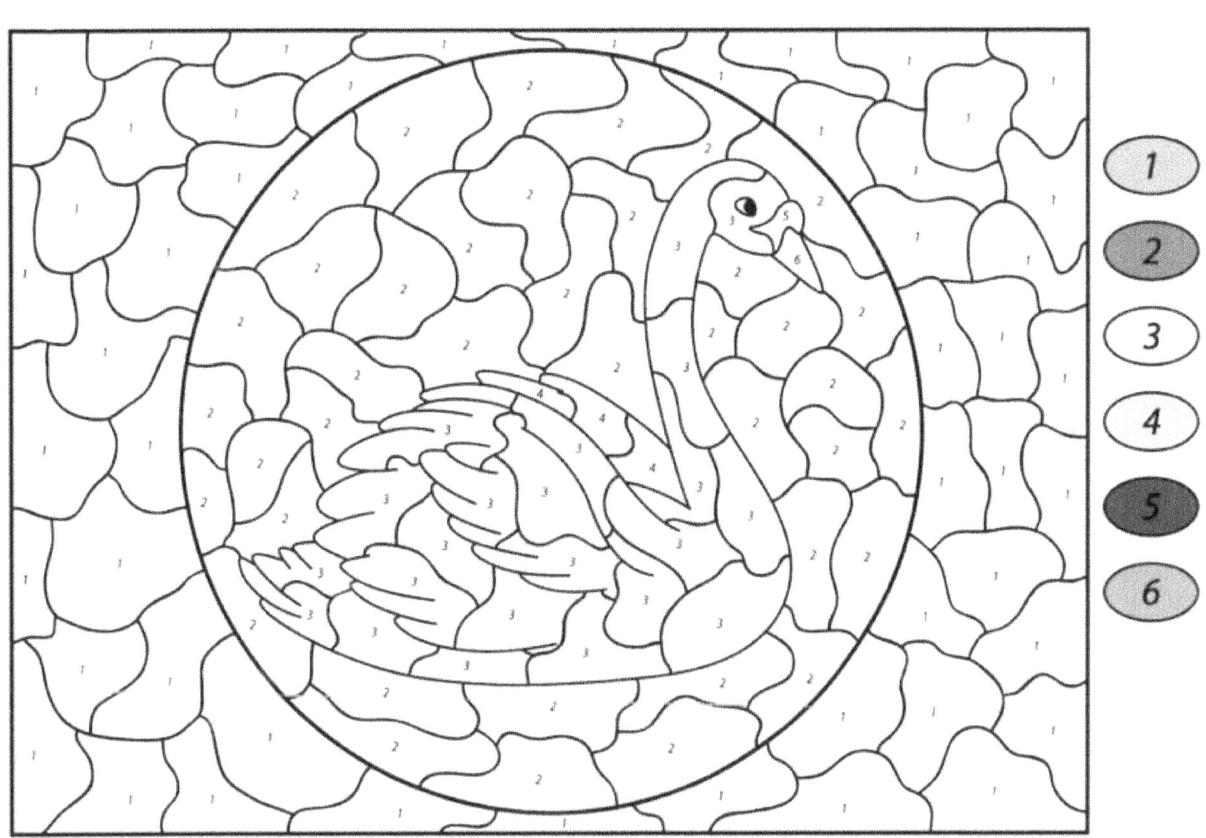

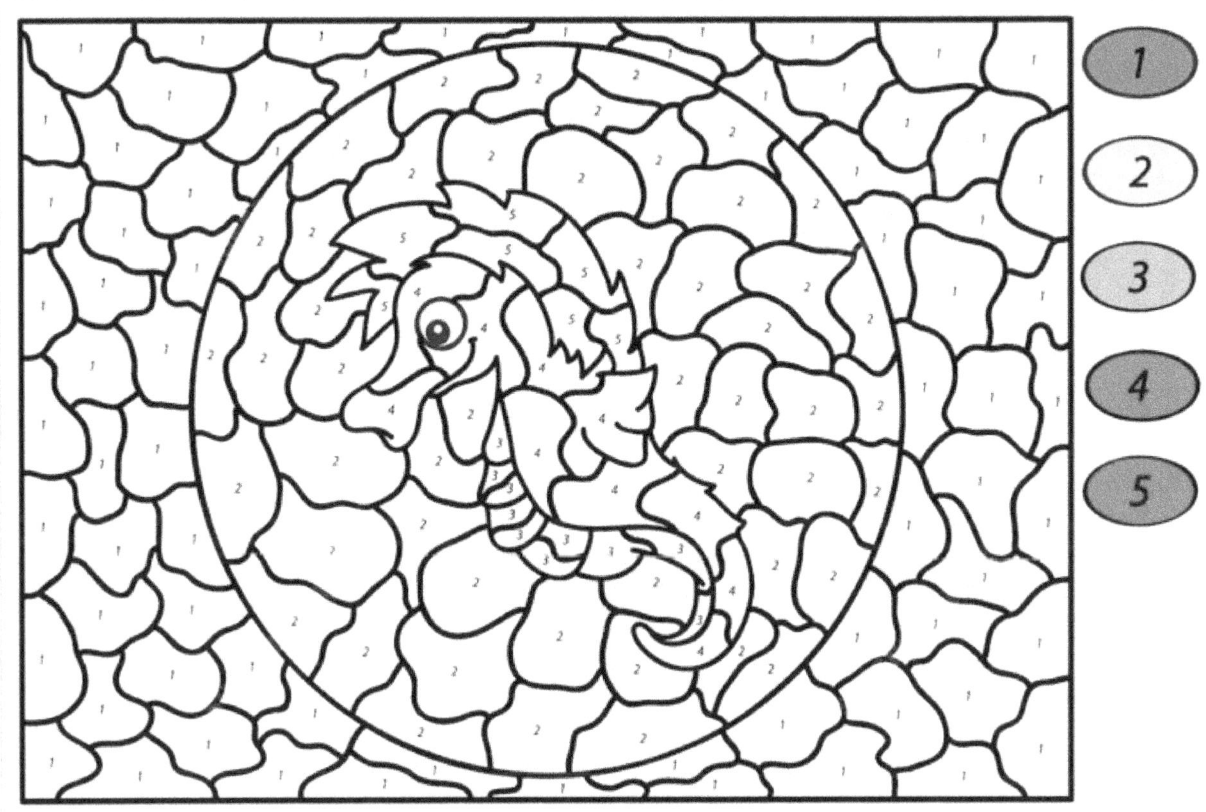

1
2
3
4
5

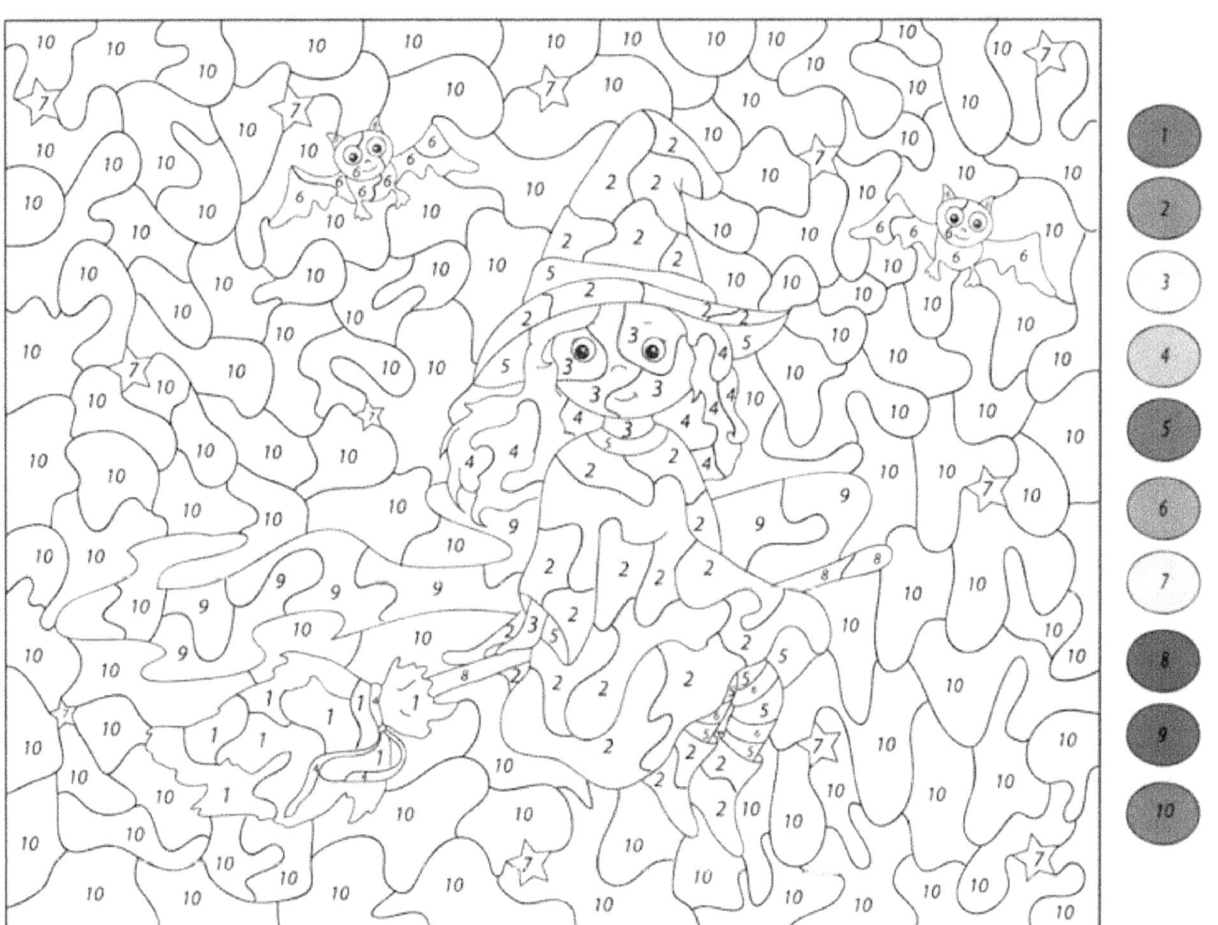

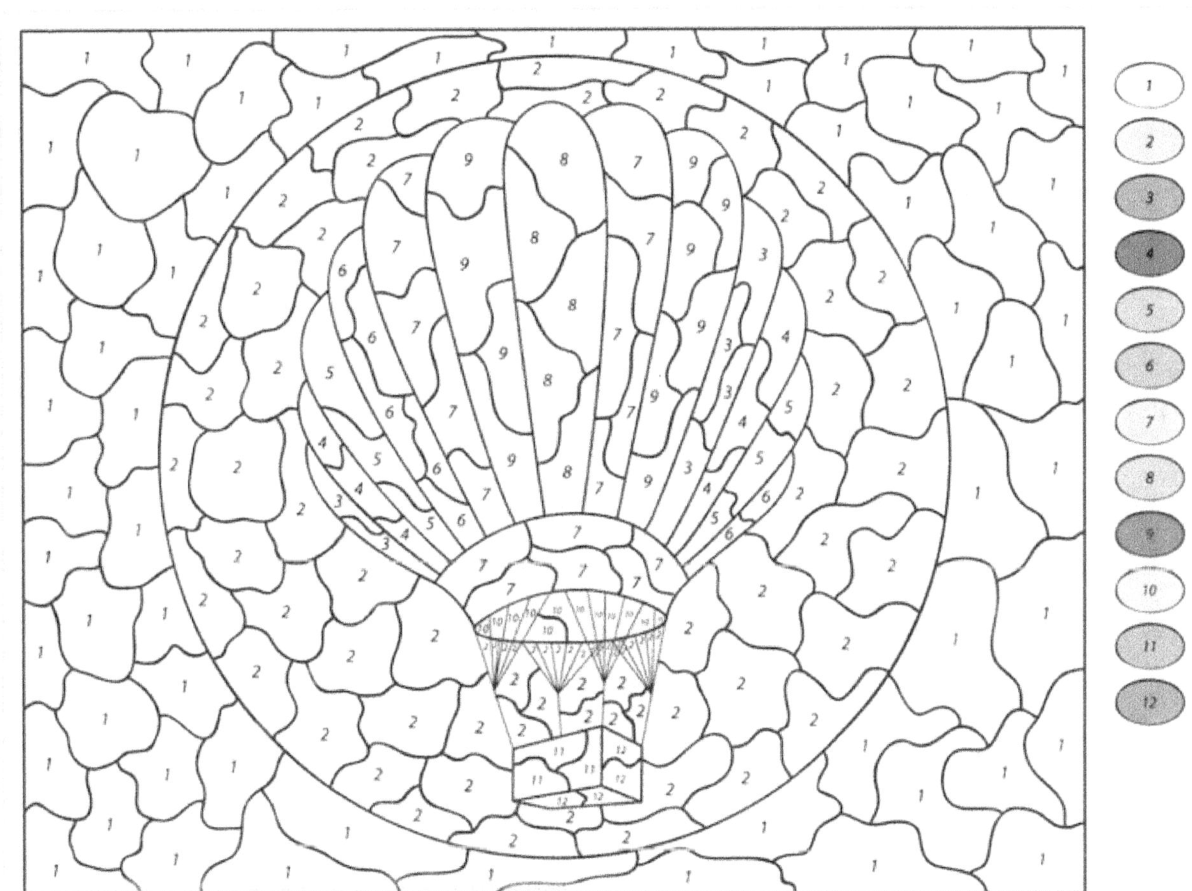

1-light green   2-dark green   3-white   4-yellow
5-orange   6-pink   7-*purple*

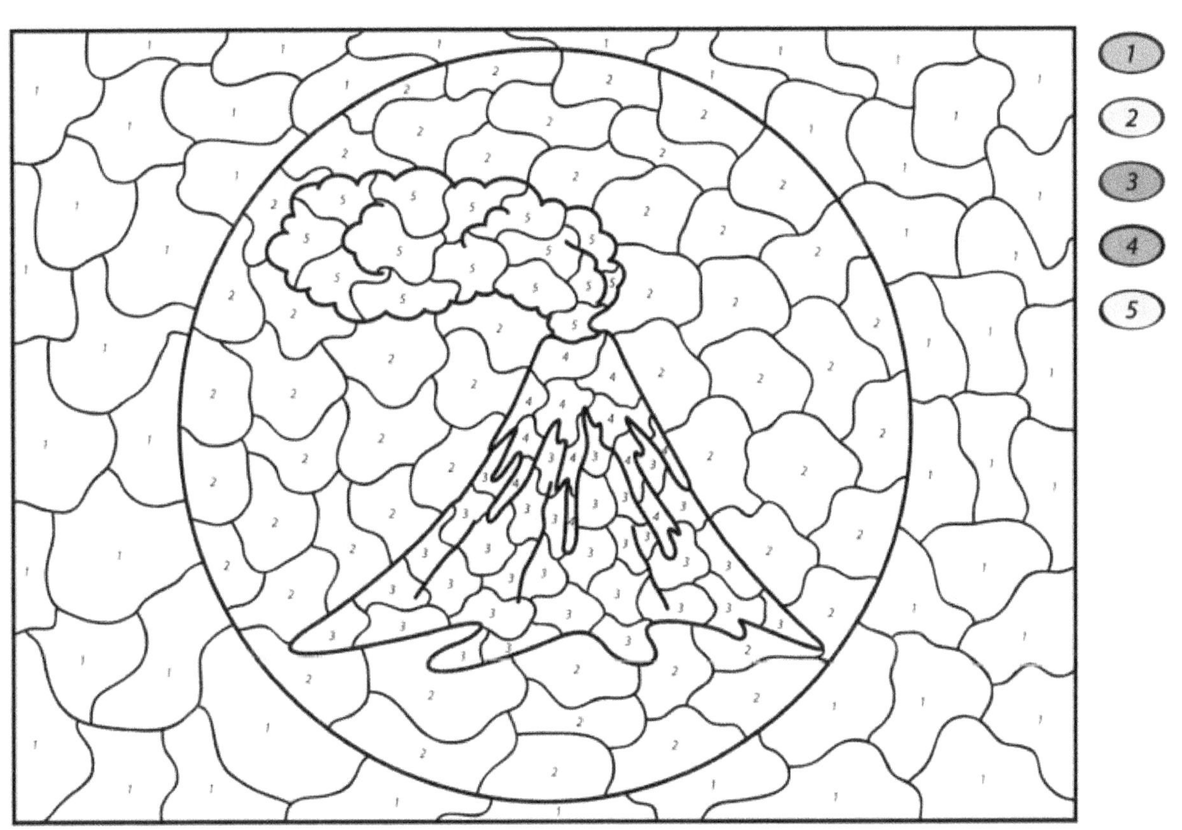

www.ingramcontent.com/pod-product-compliance
Lightning Source LLC
Chambersburg PA
CBHW080851250726
48663CB00003B/413